Between Rock and a Hard Place

More Cartoons by Pat Oliphant

Andrews, McMeel & Parker
A Universal Press Syndicate Affiliate
Kansas City • New York

Foreword

People believe that because what Pat Oliphant does is called political *cartooning*, he's poking fun at things. Fact of the matter he's not: He's deadly serious. Fact of the matter is he's a mean SOB who has been endowed with the sort of glorious sense of outrage we all should have when we see the self-important panjandrums in control of this planet running amok. Fact of the matter is, we should all be out there on the barricades with Oliphant, screaming that we're mad as hell and we're not gonna take it anymore.

Oliphant doesn't take it anymore. And we're all the richer for it.

What I like best about him is the way he gives it to everybody. Some of my more self-righteous Jewish friends think he's anti-Semitic because of the way he stuck it to Menachem Begin and Ariel Sharon during the Israeli invasion of Lebanon back in 1982. (These are the kinds of people, I should add, who put "Shiksas Are for Practice" bumper stickers on their cars.) Oliphant doesn't hate Jews — there's not a prejudiced bone in his body. He simply has an abiding disgust for liars and cheats of every ethnic, racial, and national persuasion, including — small wonder — Israeli politicians who scream "Blood libel" when they're caught with their hands in the wrong cookie jar — or in 1982, the wrong Palestinian refugee camps.

He got in trouble with Italians for the way he treated the Zaccaros, too. You remember the Zaccaros — John and Geraldine. He's in real estate; she did a Pepsi commercial. Oliphant used a lot of "Whaddayou? Whaddayou?" dialect when he drew them. And people probably thought he had it in for everyone whose name ends in a vowel. He didn't: He only had it in for John and Geraldine. They probably deserved it.

In fact, Oliphant is one of the original proponents of equal rights. Liberals and conservatives, commies and capitalists, Democrats, Republicans, homosexuals, clerics (liberal-neoconservative-commie-homosexual clerics when he can find 'em) — you name it, he's skewered them all.

How he got so mean is a subject of some discussion. We who know and love him have decided that the root cause is the fact that he was born in Australia, and spent too many years upside down burbling, "Throw another shrimp on the barbie, mate," or some such rot.

These days he's doing his daily skewering in more than 500 newspapers, courtesy of Universal Press Syndicate. I wish we had Oliphant here in Washington on a daily basis. It would prevent us from taking ourselves too seriously. It would be an antidote to all the stuff we in the national press are writing about each other and about the inmates who are running the asylum.

We watch Dan Rather and Tom Brokaw and Peter Jennings and think we're getting the whole story. We're not. We sit in our living rooms watching the TV, getting blitzed with factoids and info-bits and visual wallpaper, and we're not screaming back at the screen as we should be. We're not outraged enough.

Thank God Pat Oliphant is.

— JOHN WEISMAN

Weisman is Washington, D.C., bureau chief of *TV Guide* magazine. His new novel, *Blood Cries*, will be published in May 1987.

June 6, 1985

Spies, spies, spies . . . *

*This and all other postscripts by Pat Oliphant.

6

June 6, 1985

'CUT!'

LIGHTS! CAMERA! TEFLON!

'HERE WE ARE, LIVE, WITH MR. ZEKE CRUMLIN, WHOSE ELDER HALF-SISTER WAS ONCE MARRIED TO A THIRD COUSIN OF ONE OF THE BEIRUT HOSTAGES.... SIR, TELL US HOW YOU ARE COPING IN THIS CRISIS.''

WHAT'S BLACK AND TAN AND LOOKS GOOD ON A TV PERSON?

A DOBER MAN?

Robert Stethem, a hostage, was murdered by terrorists during a hijacking in Beirut.

July 3, 1985

July 5, 1985

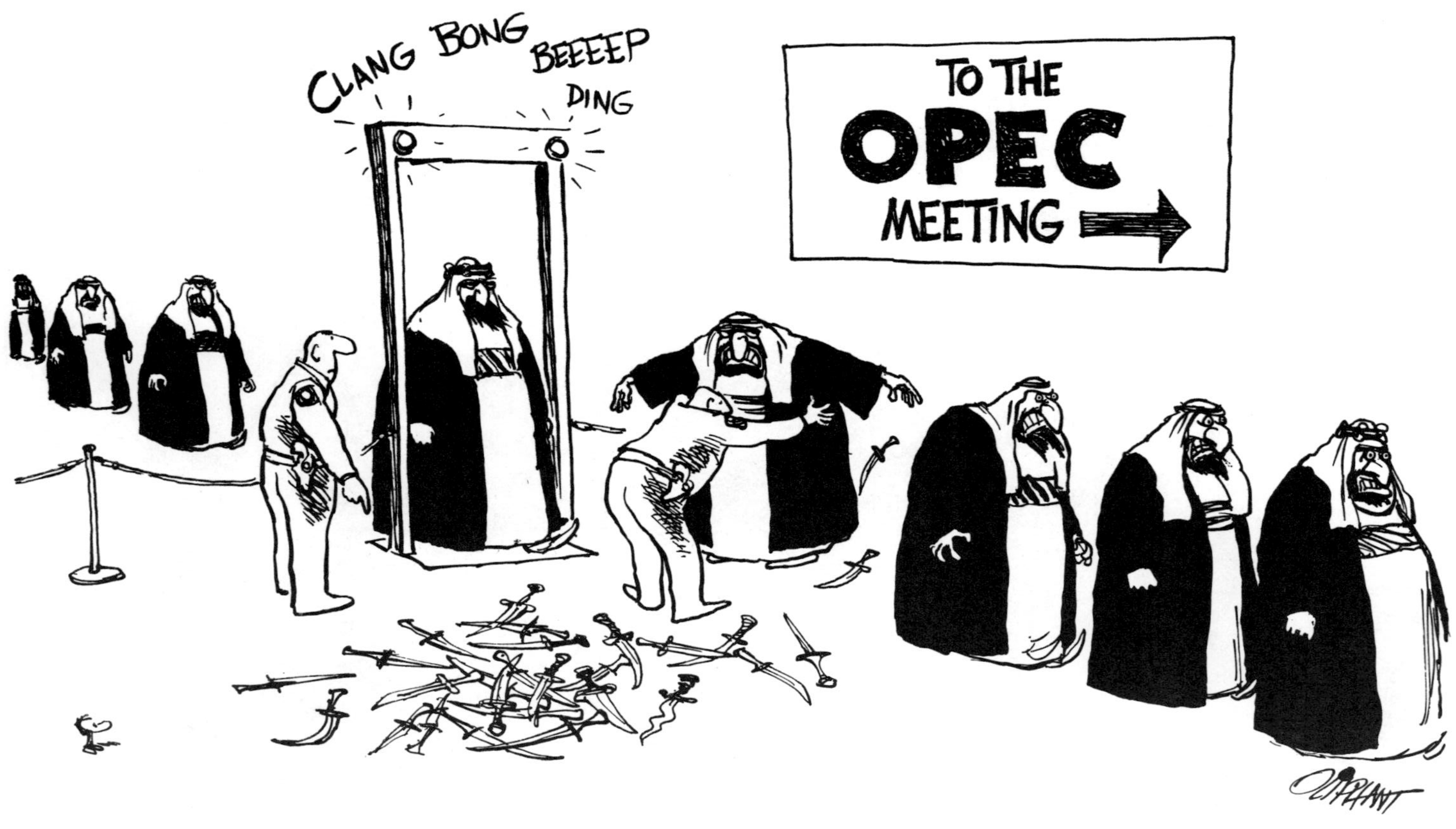

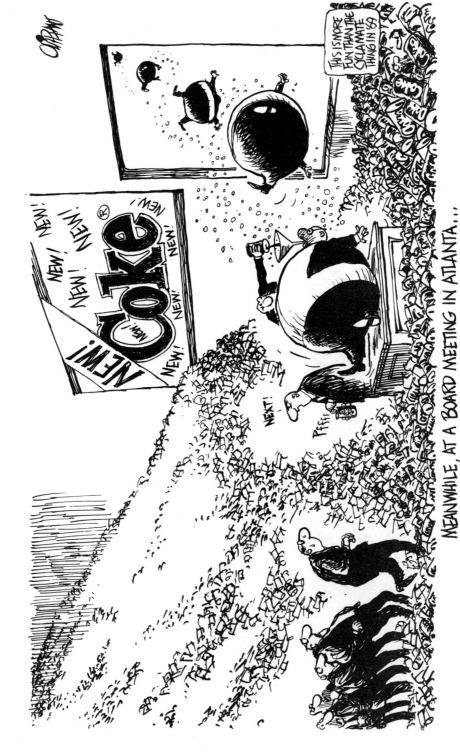

"...COMING TO YOU LIVE FROM THE PRESIDENT'S LARGE INTESTINE!"

The president is operated on for colon cancer. TV takes you there.

July 16, 1985

July 17, 1985

'HEY, TERRIFIC—MAKING BOOK ON MY RECOVERY CHANCES—I'LL HAVE SOME OF THAT!'

'COULD YOU PLEASE GET BACK IN THE BOTTLE, SIR?'

40 Years From Trinity

July 17, 1985

17

July 22, 1985

18

A STATE OF EMERGENCY

July 23, 1985

July 24, 1985

"You may be interested in our Three Mile Island model, President Li — it comes with automatic population control."

Chinese President Li shops for U.S. nuclear assistance.

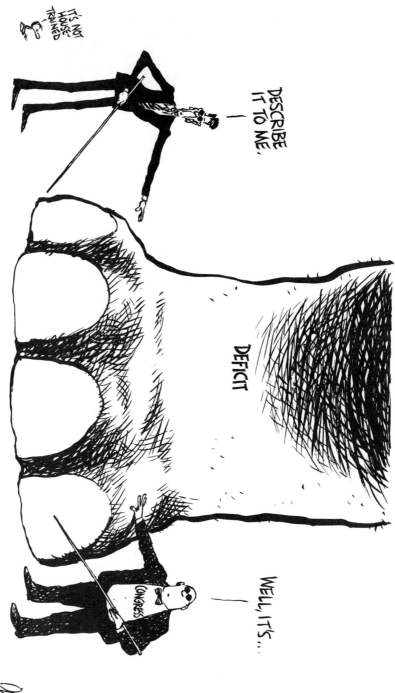

July 30, 1985

HOUNDED RELENTLESSLY ON APARTHEID BY THE REAGAN ADMINISTRATION, SOUTH AFRICA HAS WITHDRAWN ITS AMBASSADOR TO THE U.S.

July 31, 1985

23

August 1, 1985

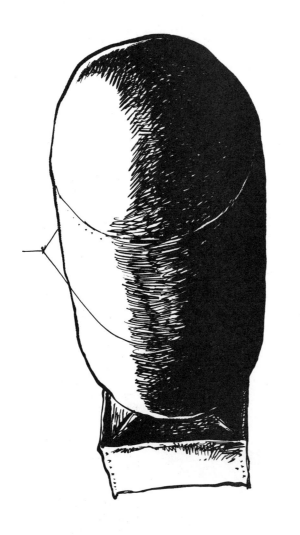

'ACTUALLY, AFTER FORTY YEARS, I RARELY GIVE IT A THOUGHT...'

An anniversary — The Bomb at 40

August 6, 1985

August 7, 1985

NATIONAL BASEBALL FANS ASSN.

HARDBALL — NO MORE MR. NICEGUY!

'WE'RE ON STRIKE AND WE'RE GONNA STAY ON STRIKE FOR AS LONG AS IT TAKES TO FORCE THE OWNERS AND PLAYERS TO COME TO AN AGREEMENT.'

28

BASEBALL—PART 3
THE OWNERS AND
PLAYERS CUT A DEAL...

August 8, 1985

August 14, 1985

August 14, 1985

August 15, 1985

August 19, 1985

Blacks beat up on blacks in South Africa.

'THE INMATES ARE HAPPY, THE CONDITIONS ARE EXCELLENT, AND THE MAN IN CHARGE IS A VERY NICE GUY—AND A FINE CONSERVATIVE, I MIGHT ADD.'

August 22, 1985

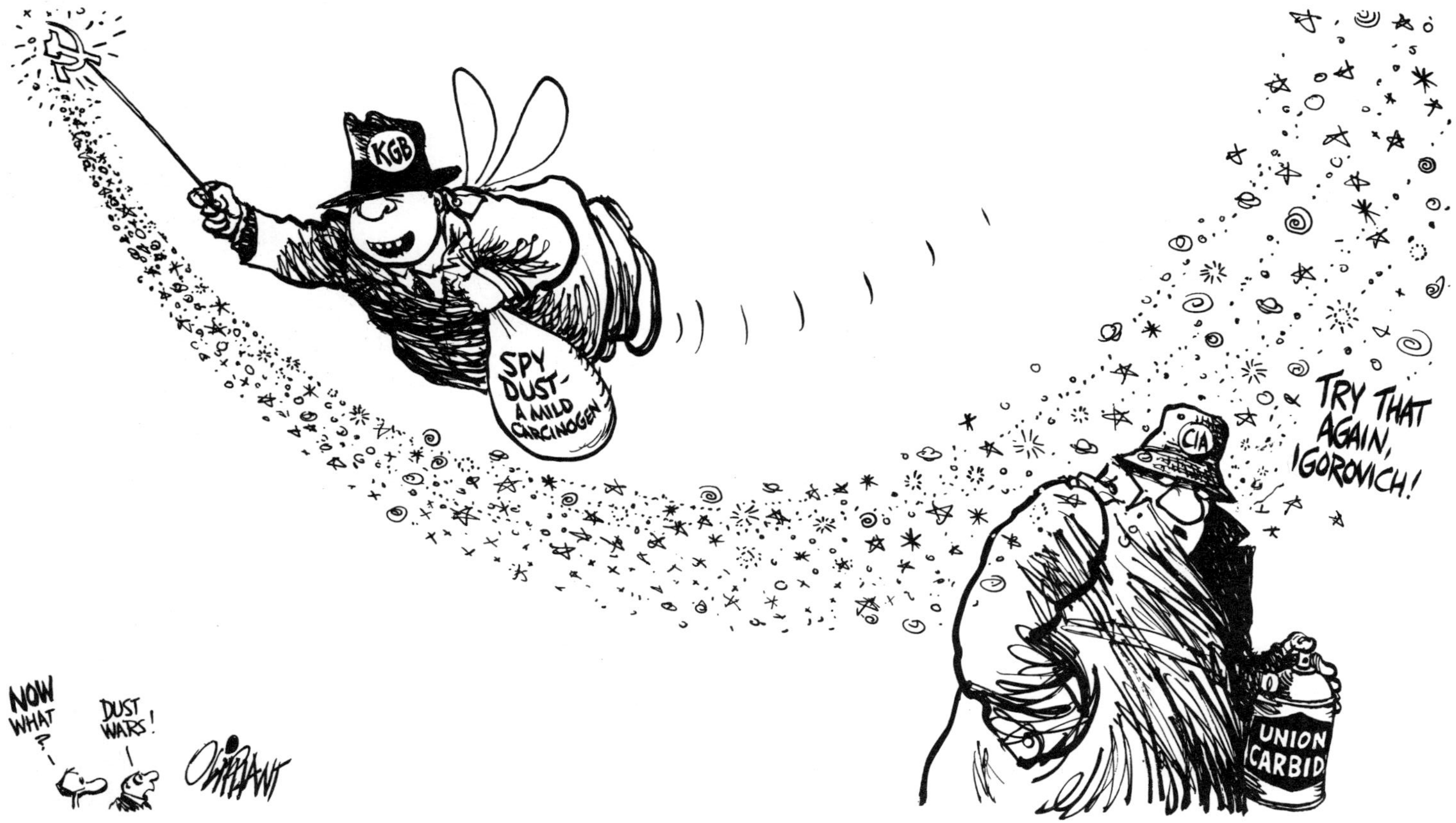

August 21, 1985

ONE FINAL TEST BEFORE WE TALK...

August 23, 1985

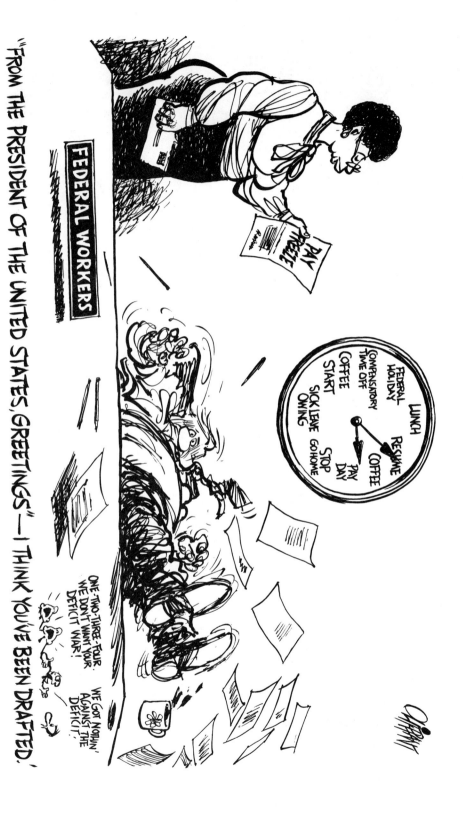

"FROM THE PRESIDENT OF THE UNITED STATES, GREETINGS"—I THINK YOU'VE BEEN DRAFTED."

August 30, 1985

September 3, 1985

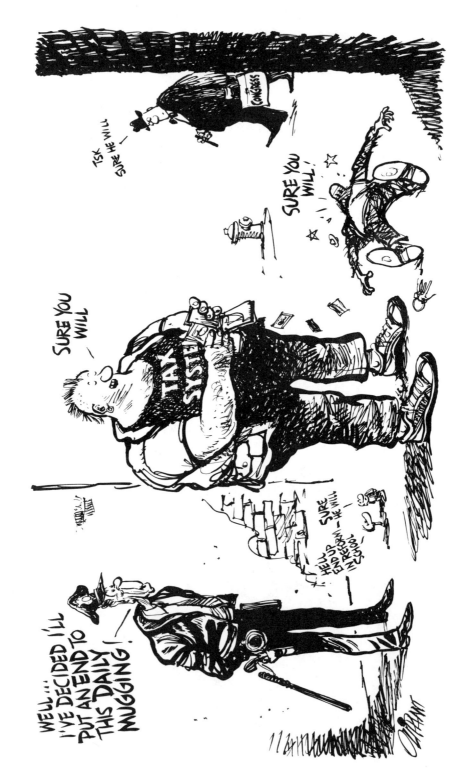

REAGAN WANTS ACCESS TO SOVIET TELEVISION.

September 10, 1985

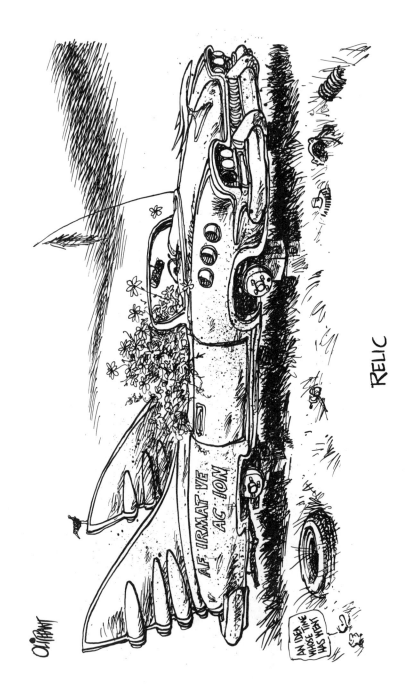

September 13, 1985

PROTECTIONISM

FORTRESS AMERICA

PROTECTION AGAINST WHAT? ALL YU DAM' CONSUMERS!

September 17, 1985

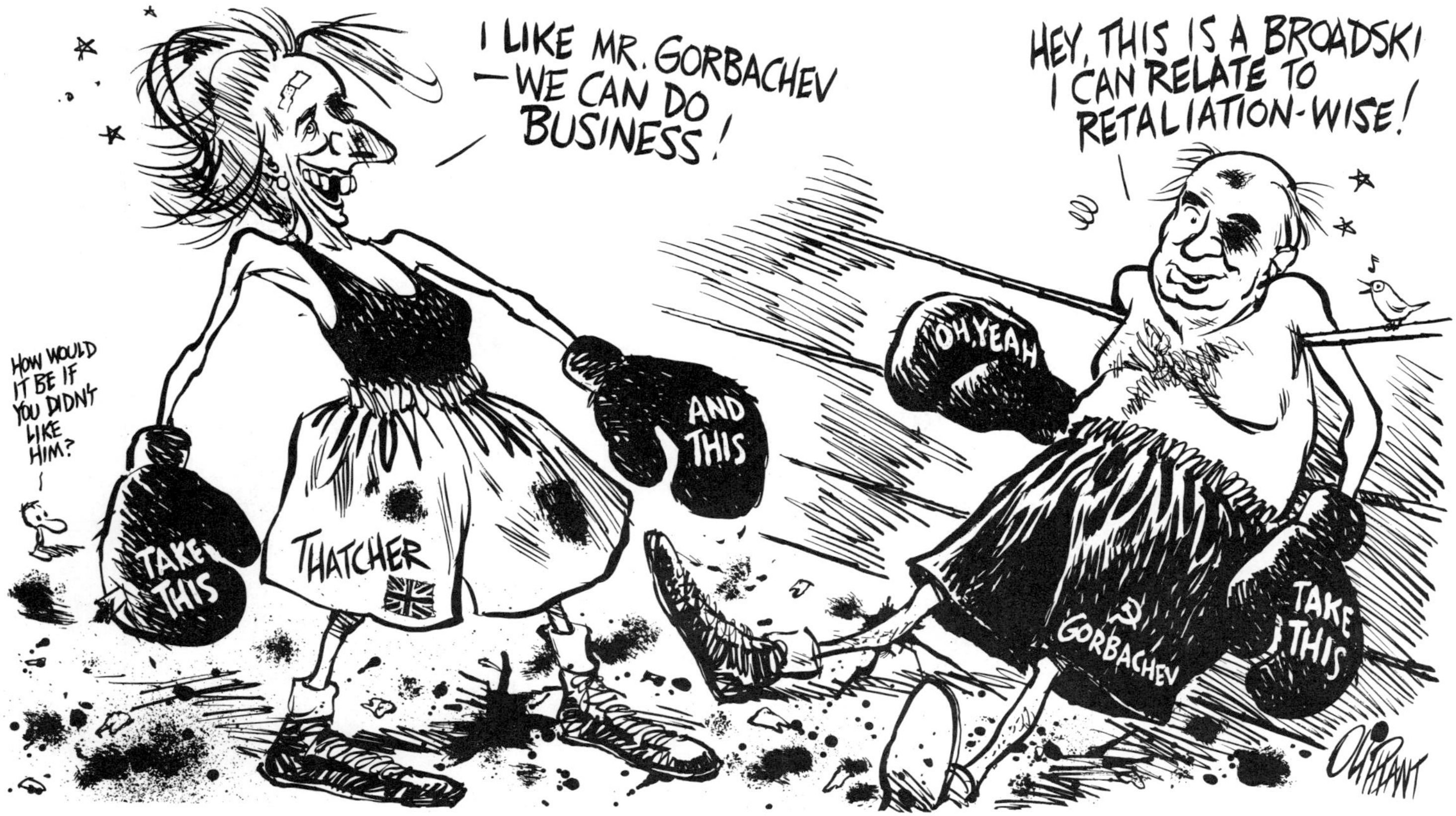

THE LADIES OF THE CLEAN MUSIC, QUILTING AND PORN WATCH SOCIETY DISCOVER YET ANOTHER DISGUSTING ROCK LYRIC.

September 20, 1985

September 23, 1985

French frogmen sink Greenpeace vessel in New Zealand. How much did Mitterrand know?

'PLEASED TO BE OF ASSISTANCE — AND NOW, MY BANKER WOULD LIKE TO TALK TO YOU ABOUT YOUR DELINQUENT MORTGAGE PAYMENTS.'

A disastrous earthquake in Mexico, and other ill-timed events.

September 24, 1985

September 25, 1985

'TELL HIM WE JUST WANT TO SING HIM SOME NICE SONGS ABOUT HARD TIMES DOWN ON THE FARM.'

September 26, 1985

October 1, 1985

56

For what must be the first time, Russian personnel are the victims of terrorism.

October 2, 1985

57

OUR POLICY BULLETIN BOARD

'SOME SLICKED-UP RUSSIAN TAPDANCER SAYS HE'S COME TO TAKE YOU AWAY FROM ALL THIS, MY DEAR.'

October 7, 1985

THE OTHER APARTHEID

THE NEGATIVE AFFIRMATIVE!

AFFIRMATIVE ACTION!

'IF I KNEW WHO WAS RESPONSIBLE, I WOULD PUNISH THEM MYSELF!'

October 14, 1985

October 17, 1985

Egypt allows the Achille Lauro hijackers to escape.

'HIJACKED AN ITALIAN SHIP, MURDERED AN ELDERLY JEW IN A WHEELCHAIR, REINFORCED U.S.-ISRAELI RELATIONS, INCREASED THE CLIMATE OF VIOLENCE FURTHER... MY, MY, WHAT ELSE DID YOU DO TO US?'

October 23, 1985

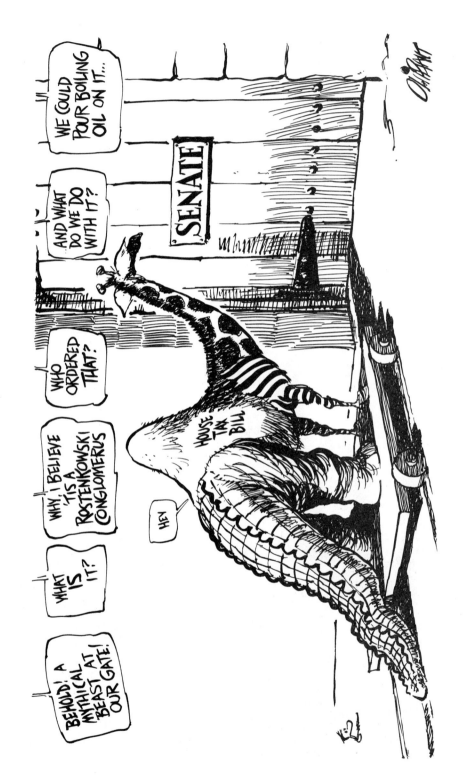

October 29, 1985

October 30, 1985

72

AIDS SCARE BRINGS NEW GUILD RULINGS ON SCREEN KISSING—

November 4, 1985

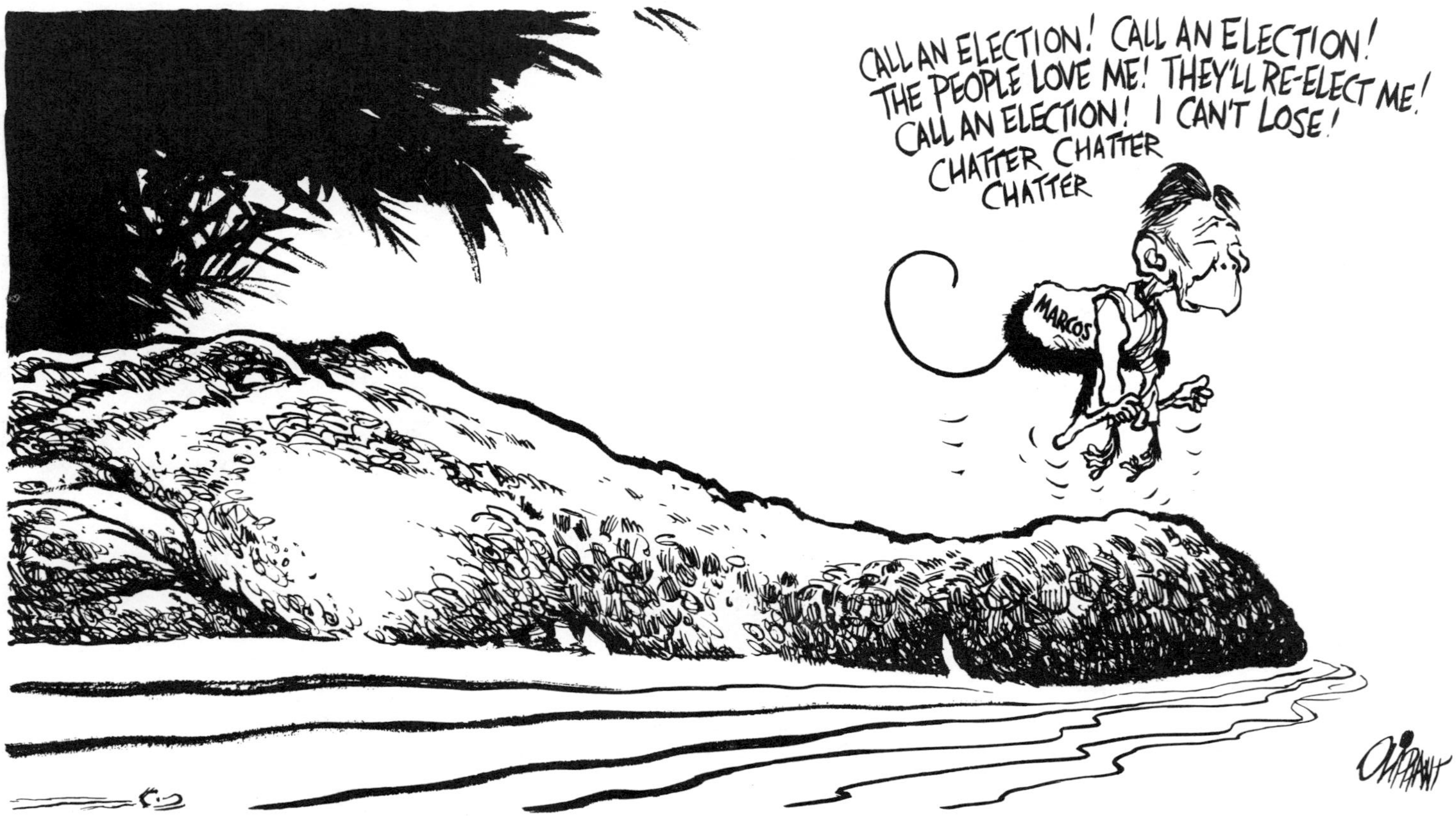

November 5, 1985

The CIA loses a defector, who leaves a restaurant in D.C. to redefect to the Soviet Embassy.

THE SAGA CONTINUES — 3 REHABILITATED DEFECTORS EXCHANGE NOTES.

November 8, 1985

A royal visit to the U.S.

November 11, 1985

NATIONAL ZOO
PANDA
EXPECTING

CONGRATULATIONS —
SO AM I!

GENEVA

WE'LL BE BACK AFTER
THIS PREGNANT PAUSE
FROM OUR SPONSOR...

November 21, 1985

'ASYLUM? WHAT ASYLUM? SPEAK ENGLISH, BOY—ALL I CAN HEAR IS GOBBLE GOBBLE GOBBLE!'

A Russian seaman attempting to defect is returned to his ship by INS officers who can't understand him. Then came Thanksgiving . . .

Terrorist pursuit, Egyptian style

How did you do that?

ROSTENKOWSKI

TAX BILL

November 27, 1985

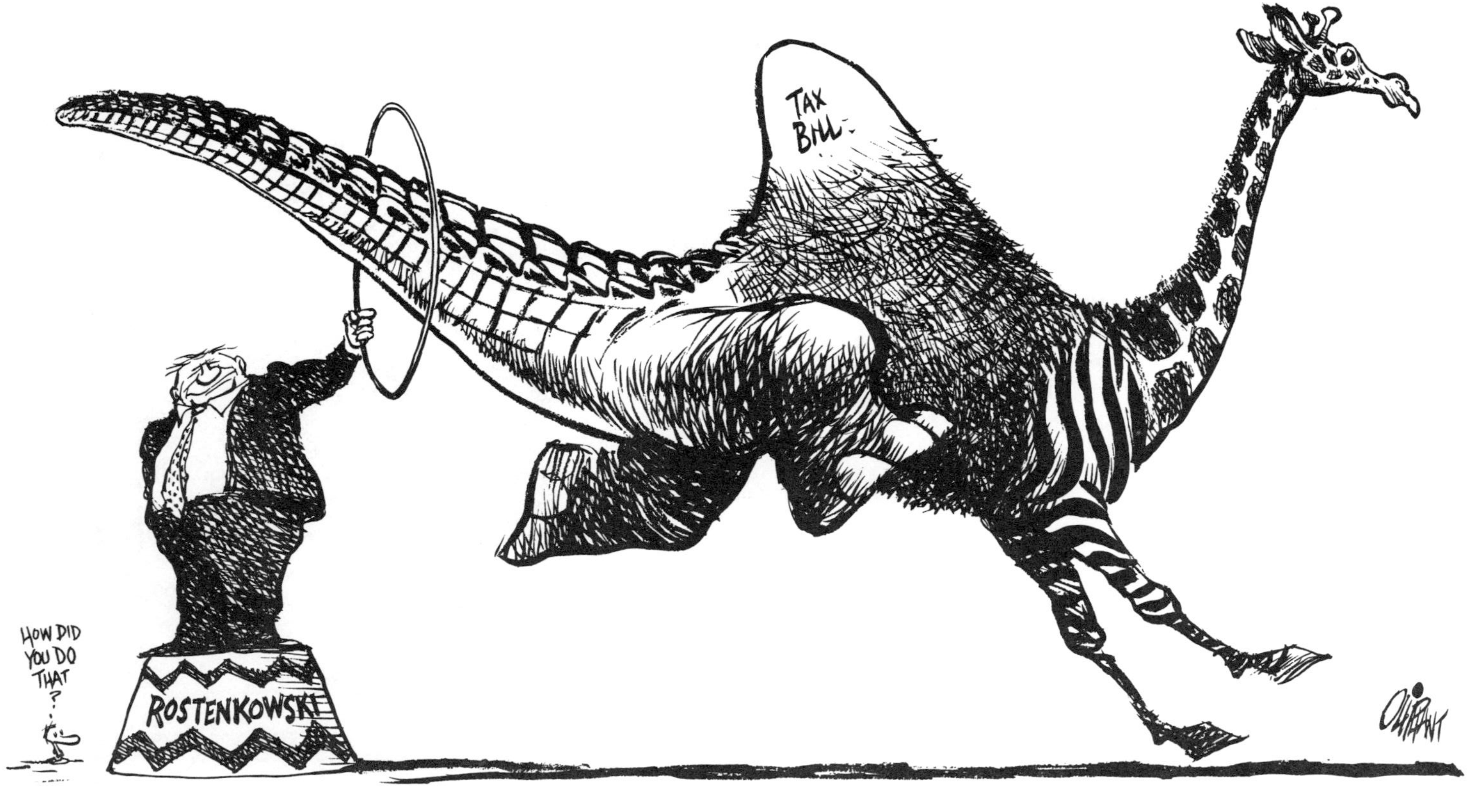

November 29, 1985

Israel spies on the U.S.

December 3, 1985

The Real President stands up.

December 4, 1985

December 5, 1985

December 6, 1985

December 11, 1985

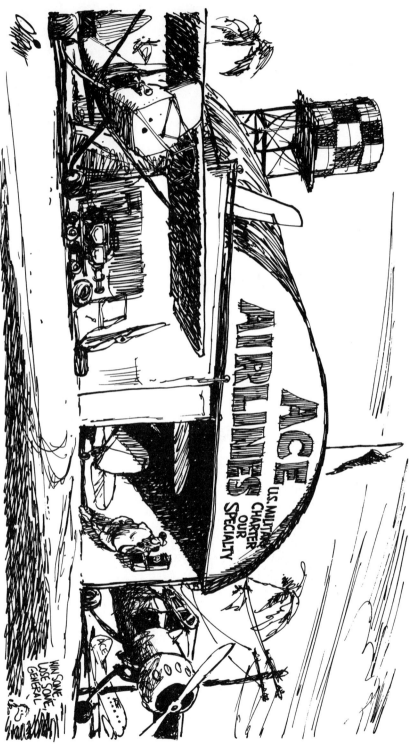

"WHY, HOWDY, GENERAL ... SURE, WE CAN FLY YOUR ARMY ANY PLACE ... WHY, YESSIR, WE DO UNDERSTAND YOU GOTTA CUT COSTS, SO WE'LL GIVE YOU PENTAGON BOYS A GOOD PRICE ..."

December 18, 1985

December 18, 1985

..., AND BEHOLD, IT CAME TO PASS THAT THEY ALL WENT UP UNTO THE LAND OF THE SENATE,

December 20, 1985

December 26, 1985

JOSEPH CHECKS THE BILLS — AN APRÈS-CHRISTMAS TRADITION IS BORN....

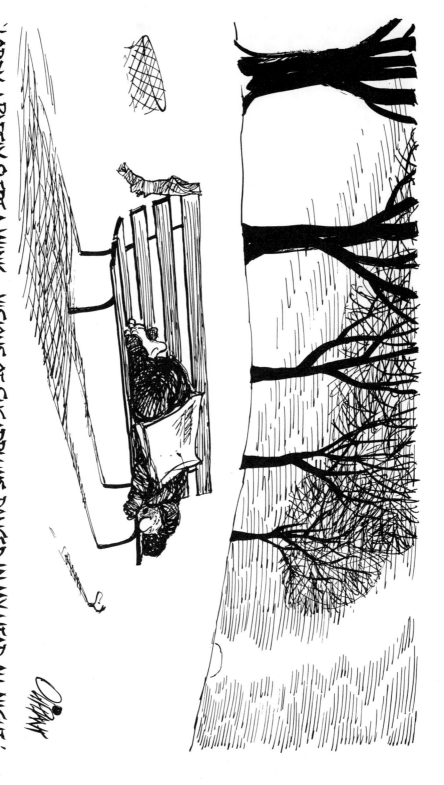

'LORDY, I BARELY SLEPT A WINK — VISIONS OF SUGARPLUMS DANCED IN MY HEAD ALL NIGHT.'

Christmas morning in disadvantage-land

December 23, 1985

101

"WELCOME BACK, SIR. WHILE YOU WERE AWAY, OUR COMPANY ABSORBED YOUR COMPANY, MAKING YOU NOW PART OF MEGASIGMACORP, A SUBSIDIARY OF DYNAMAX WORLDWIDE, INC.'

Mergers, mergers . . . .

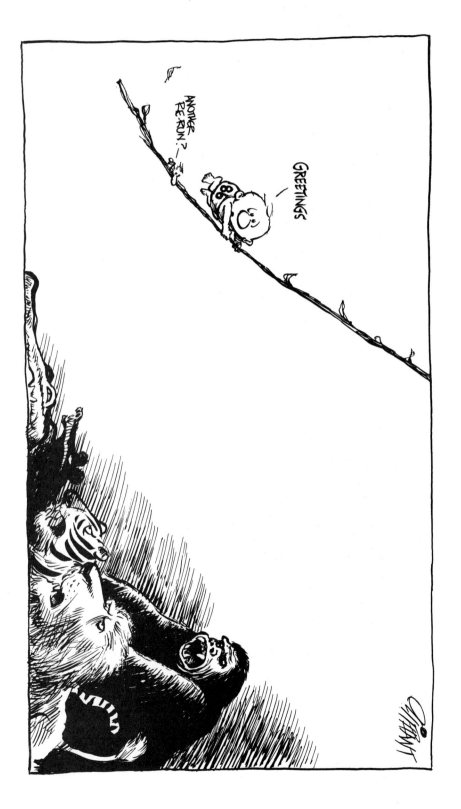

Happy New Year!

December 30, 1985

'STEP OUT OF THE CAR, SIR.'

TERRORISM

GADDAFI

IT'S LINE-
WALKIN' TIME
FOR MUAMMAR

December 31, 1985

January 2, 1986

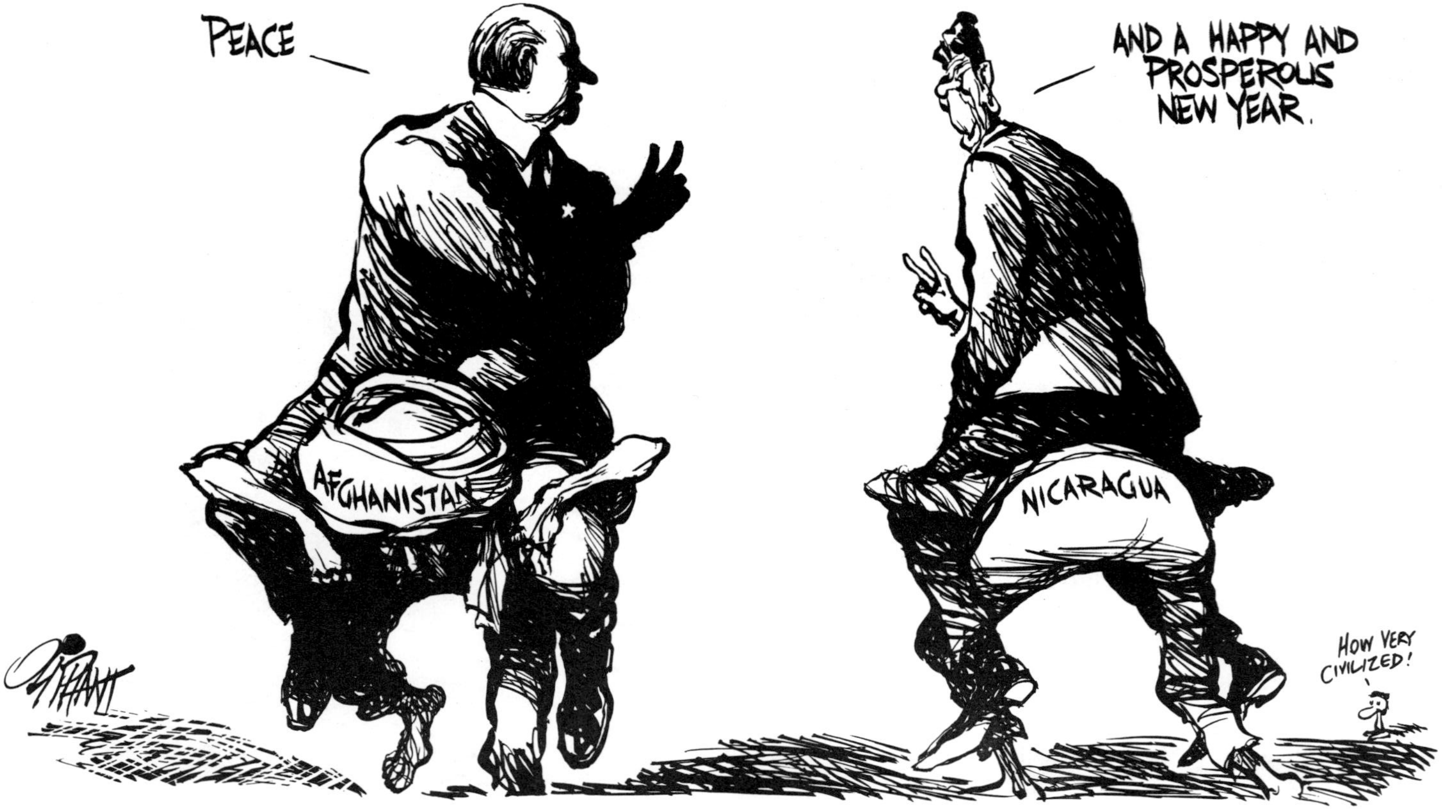

January 6, 1986

U.S. calls for sanctions against Libya in anti-terrorist move.

A ROSE
IS A ROSE
IS A ROSE

FALWELL'S
~~MORAL MAJORITY~~
LIBERTY
FEDERATION

AND BY ANY
OTHER NAME
SMELLS
JUST AS
MUCH

January 10, 1986

OLIPHANT

A national holiday is proclaimed for Dr. Martin Luther King, Jr.

January 16, 1986

January 20, 1986

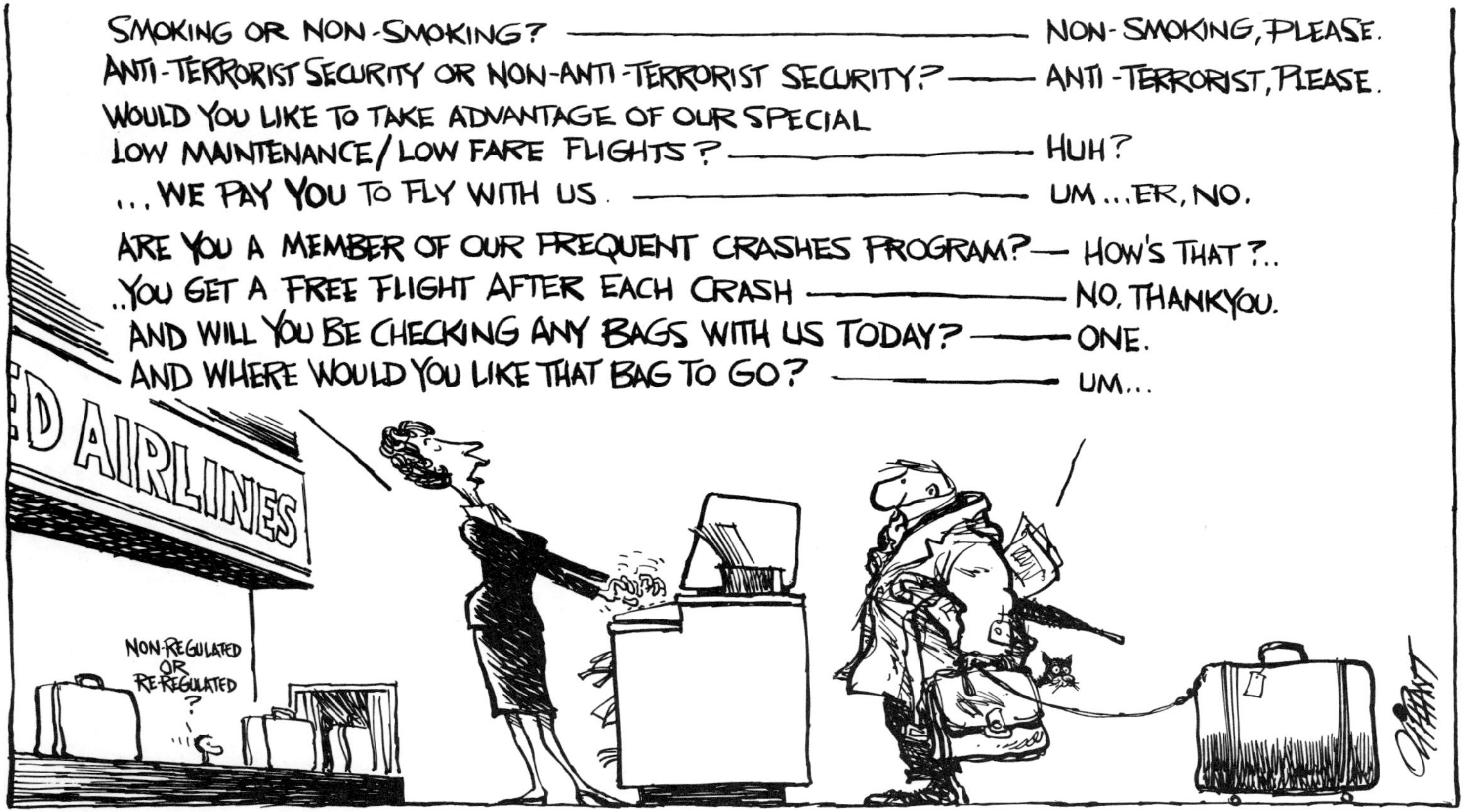

January 21, 1986

114

'HOW NICE TO GET BACK TO TRADITIONAL VALUES...'

'BANANAS? WHAT BANANAS??'

Little did we realize how many bananas the monkey had stolen.

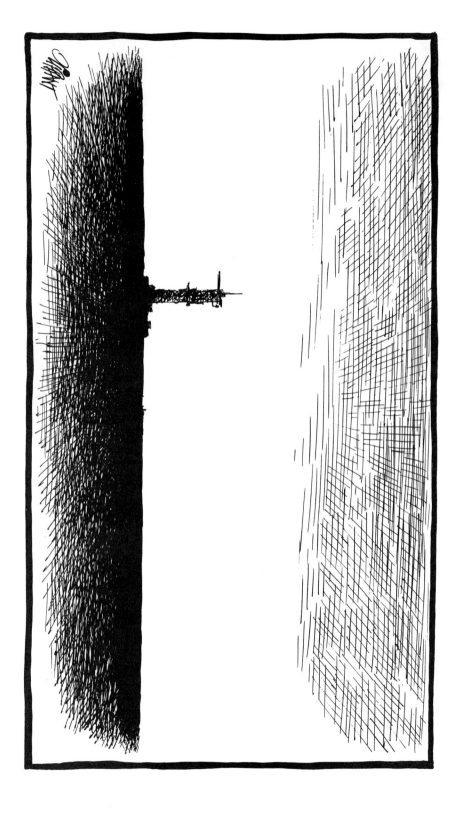

The shuttle is lost.

January 28, 1986

ALARMED BY THE MANY DANGERS, THE PIONEERS ABANDONED WESTWARD EXPLORATION EXCEPT FOR A SERIES OF UNMANNED PRAIRIE PROBE VEHICLES...

CONESTOGA 1

Luckily, NASA wasn't in charge of the launch.

January 29, 1986

February 4, 1986

February 5, 1986

C'mon listen — the man's serious.

February 6, 1986

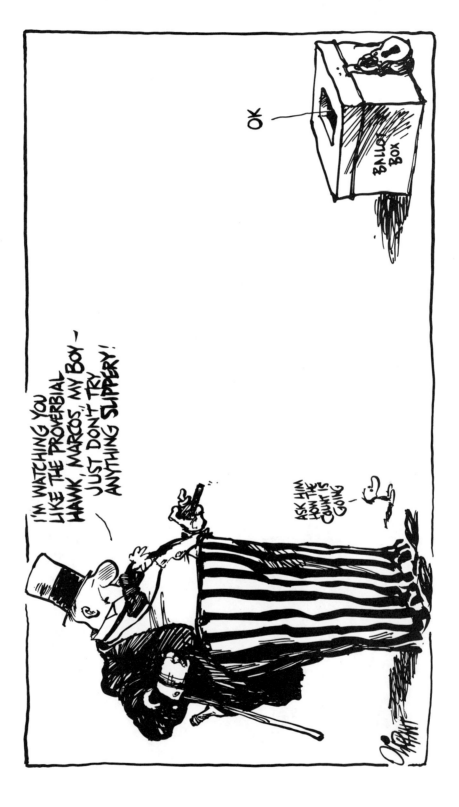

Philippine election time

February 11, 1986

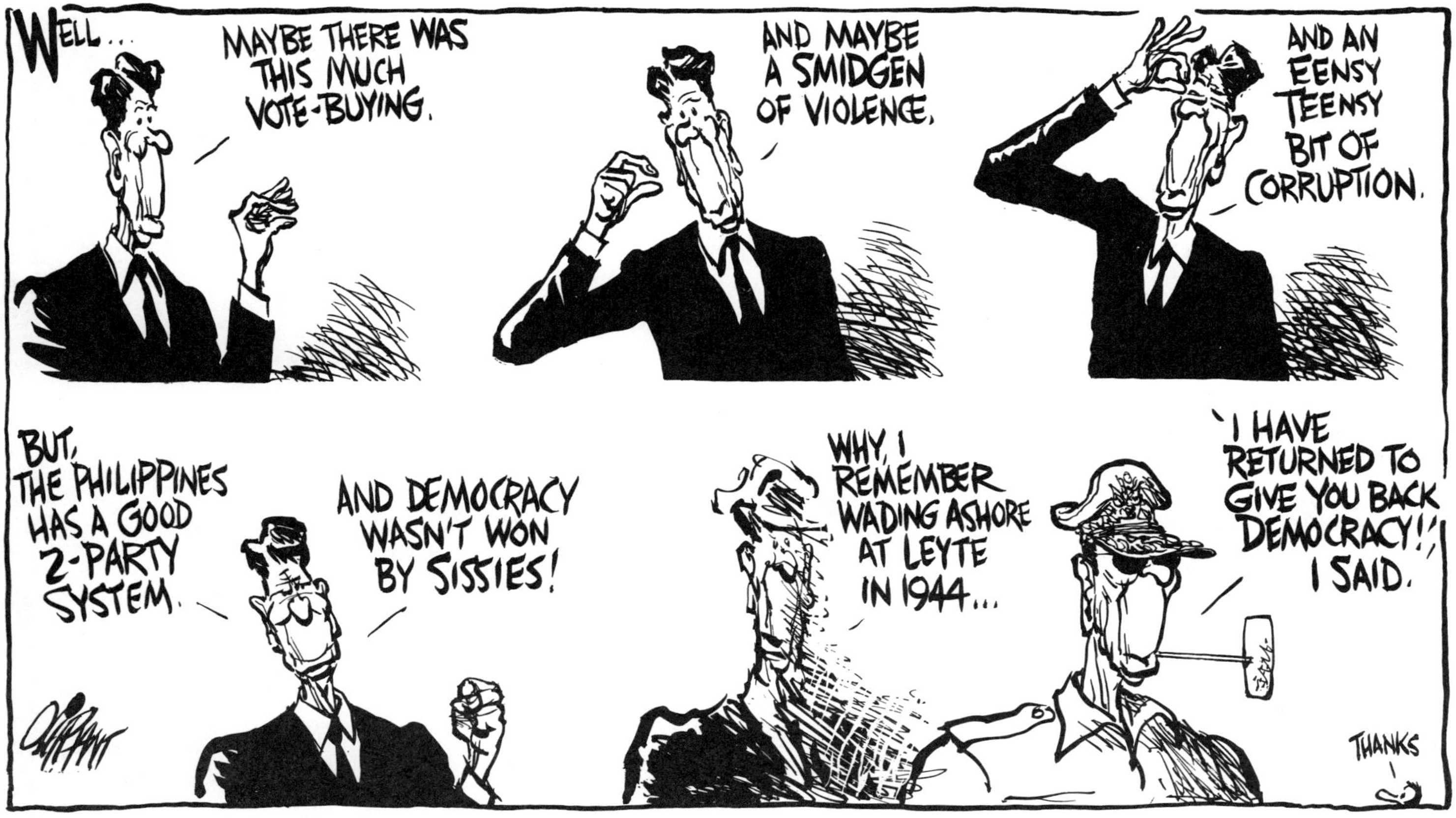

SHCHARANSKY HUMANITARIAN AWARD

TAKE A NUMBER

February 13, 1986

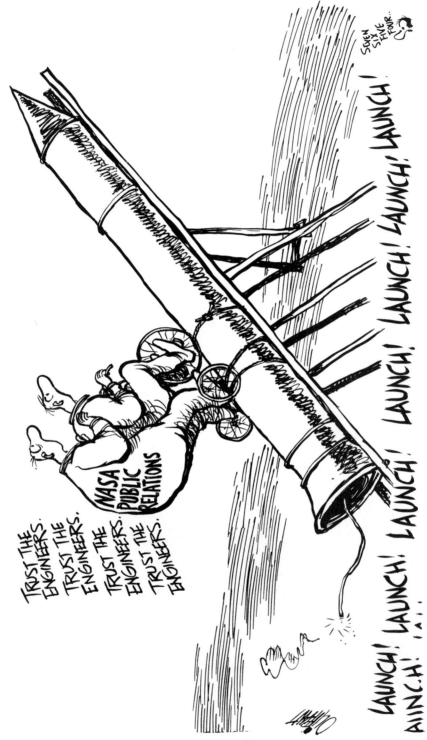

February 19, 1986

129

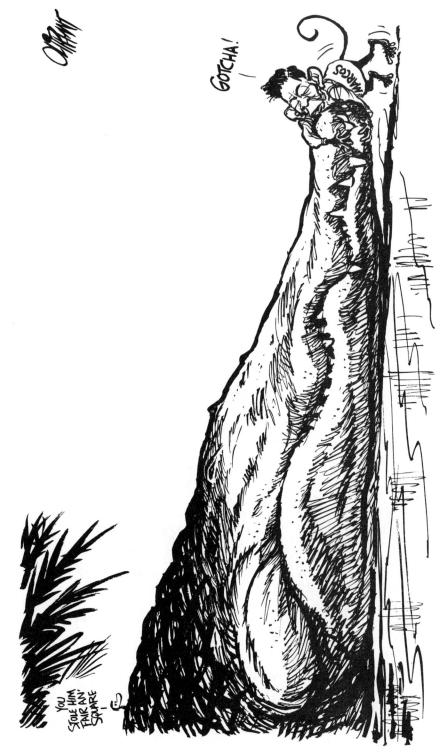

February 21, 1986

Marcos claims election victory.

130

Done and done.

February 24, 1986

Gorbachev moves to get Russia moving again.

February 26, 1986

'SIR, THIS IS NOT A SAFE AREA FOR YOU TO BE IN. PLEASE ALLOW ME TO HAND YOUR MONEY TO THIS UNIFORMED OFFICER FOR SAFE-KEEPING.'

February 28, 1986

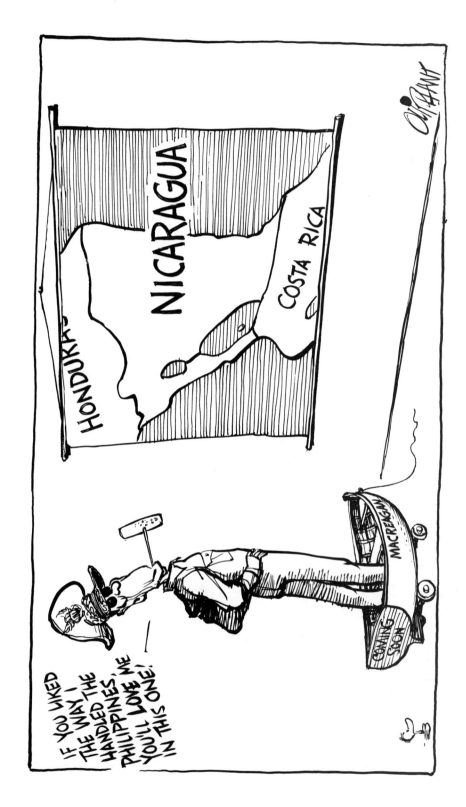

Asylum for a dictator yearning to breathe free.

March 4, 1986

ATTENTION! NOW HEAR THIS NOW HEAR THIS ALL AMERICAN WORKERS WILL REPORT FOR TESTING!

DRUG TESTING

LIE DETECTOR TESTING

APPROVED READING TESTING

MOVIE TRIVIA KNOWLEDGE TESTING

FUNDAMENTALIST CHRISTIAN RELIGION TESTING

CLEAN ROCK LYRICS TESTING

THE PRESIDENT'S S.O.B. TEST

UNIFORM ATTITUDE APTITUDE TESTING

TESTING TESTING

CONGRATULATIONS! YOU ARE NOW A 100% APPROVED REAGAN AMERICAN!

OLIPHANT

March 6, 1986

Lawyers, torts, insurance companies, premiums, big settlements, lawyers, torts, etc. . . . .

March 17, 1986

Secrets from Imelda's closet

March 19, 1986

March 20, 1986

The Marcoses search for a suitable permanent home.

March 24, 1986

145

U.S. bombs Libya.

No aid for the Nicaraguan Contras.

March 21, 1986

147

Then, Ortega attacks the Contras in Honduras . . . .

Easter again.

March 27, 1986

March 31, 1986

In Illinois, rabid right winger Lyndon LaRouche successfully launches his own Democratic candidates for lieutenant governor and secretary of state.

151

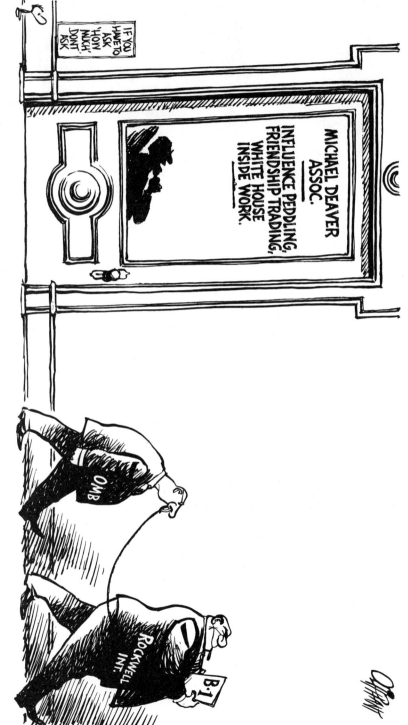

April 2, 1986

Deaver left the White House and went into business for himself.

'SORRY, COLONEL, BUT YOUR INSURANCE HAS BEEN CANCELED.'

More terrorism

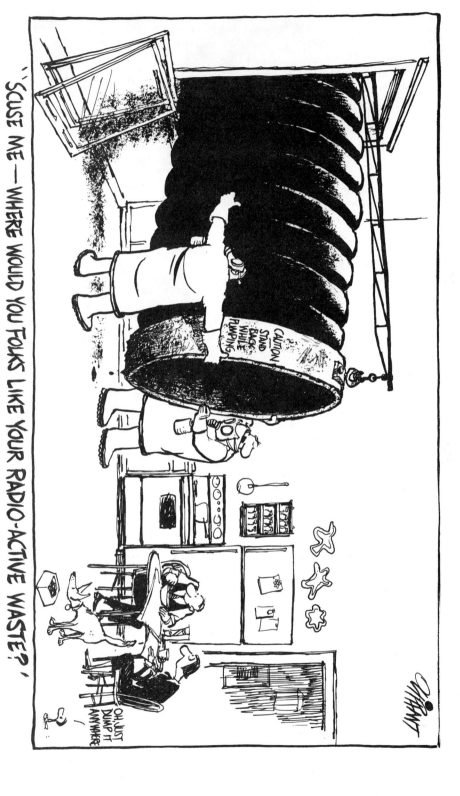

Coming, ready or not.

BUSH OF ARABIA.

DRIFTIN'

GRAMM-RUDMAN

I LIKED 'IDLE' BETTER

AN IDYLL, MR. O'NEILL

WHY ELYSIUM, MR. DOLE

April 8, 1986

ALLIES.

The Gadhafi dilemma

April 9, 1986

159

Pity the poor IRS.

April 24, 1986

April 25, 1986

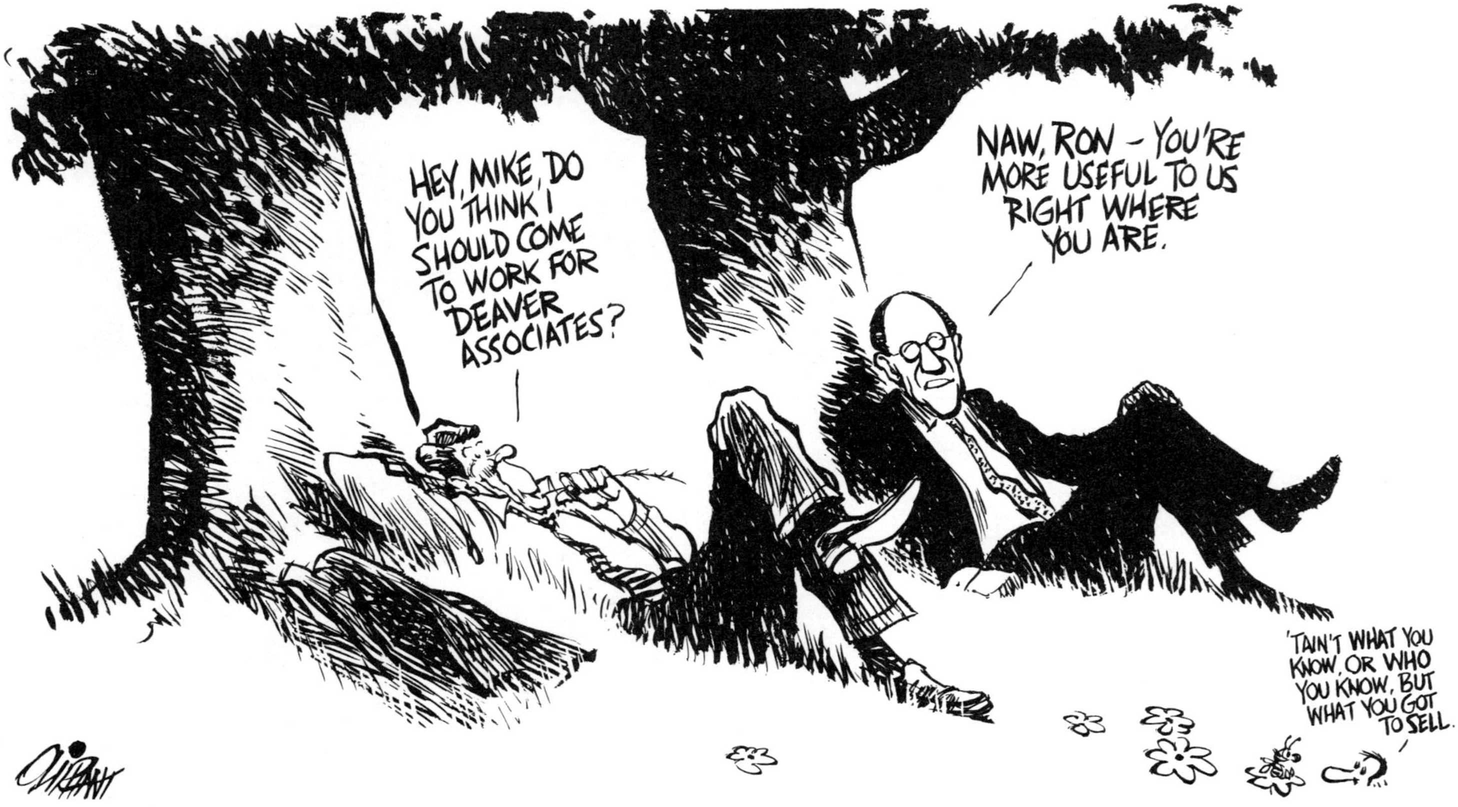

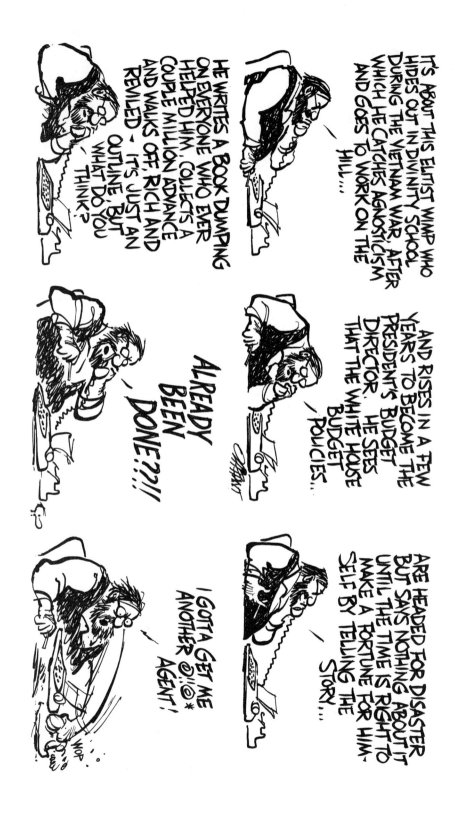

IT'S ABOUT THIS ELITIST WIMP WHO HIDES OUT IN DIVINITY SCHOOL DURING THE VIETNAM WAR, AFTER WHICH HE CATCHES AGNOSTICISM AND GOES TO WORK ON THE HILL...

AND RISES IN A FEW YEARS TO BECOME THE PRESIDENT'S BUDGET DIRECTOR. HE SEES THAT THE WHITE HOUSE BUDGET POLICIES...

ARE HEADED FOR DISASTER BUT SAYS NOTHING ABOUT IT UNTIL THE TIME IS RIGHT TO MAKE A FORTUNE FOR HIMSELF BY TELLING THE STORY...

HE WRITES A BOOK DUMPING ON EVERYONE WHO EVER HELPED HIM, COLLECTS A COUPLE MILLION ADVANCE AND WALKS OFF, RICH AND REVILED - IT'S JUST AN OUTLINE, BUT WHAT DO YOU THINK?

ALREADY BEEN DONE!?!!

I GOTTA GET ME ANOTHER @!!© * AGENT!

WOP.

Meltdown at Chernobyl

Please! Not in polite society!

April 30, 1986

More on David Stockman, recent millionaire

The Titan explodes at launch.

May 5, 1986

May 8, 1986

Kurt Waldheim, the Austrian people's choice.

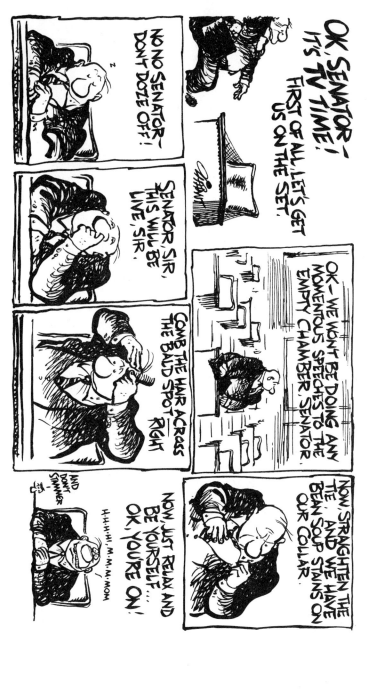

May 12, 1986

May 13, 1986

CONGRESSIONAL ARAB-BASHING

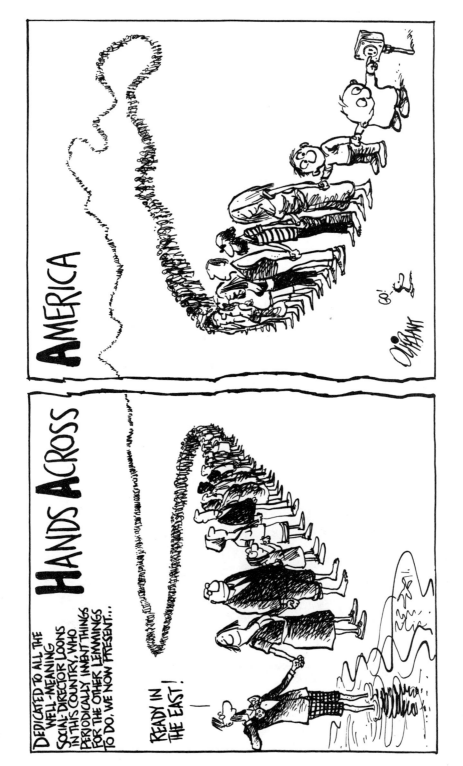

The opening of the Silly Season